YOUR NEW
GARDEN
POND

Anmarie Barrie

CONTENTS

Photos by Dr. Herbert R. Axelrod, V. Capaldi, Gary Cochran, Michael Gilroy, Burkhard Kahl, Lilypons Water Gardens, Hugh Nicholas, H. Schultz, Vincent Serbin, Jorg Vierke, and L. Wischnath.

Photos on pages 13-16 showing how to set up a pond using a flexible liner are used courtesy of Stapeley Water Gardens, Ltd., Nantwich, Cheshire, England.

9 8 7 6 5 4 3 2 1   **1996 Edition**   95 789

Distributed in the UNITED STATES to the Pet Trade by T.F.H. Publications, Inc., One T.F.H. Plaza, Neptune City, NJ 07753; distributed in the UNITED STATES to the Bookstore and Library Trade by National Book Network, Inc. 4720 Boston Way, Lanham MD 20706; in CANADA to the Pet Trade by H & L Pet Supplies Inc., 27 Kingston Crescent, Kitchener, Ontario N2B 2T6; Rolf C. Hagen Ltd., 3225 Sartelon Street, Montreal 382 Quebec; in CANADA to the Book Trade by Vanwell Publishing Ltd., 1 Northrup Crescent, St. Catharines, Ontario L2M 6P5 ; in ENGLAND by T.F.H. Publications, PO Box 15, Waterlooville PO7 6BQ; in AUSTRALIA AND THE SOUTH PACIFIC by T.F.H. (Australia), Pty. Ltd., Box 149, Brookvale 2100 N.S.W., Australia; in NEW ZEALAND by Brooklands Aquarium Ltd. 5 McGiven Drive, New Plymouth, RD1 New Zealand; in Japan by T.F.H. Publications, Japan—Jiro Tsuda, 10-12-3 Ohjidai, Sakura, Chiba 285, Japan; in SOUTH AFRICA by Lopis (Pty) Ltd., P.O. Box 39127, Booysens, 2016, Johannesburg, South Africa. Published by T.F.H. Publications, Inc.

MANUFACTURED IN THE UNITED STATES OF AMERICA
BY T.F.H. PUBLICATIONS, INC.

Introduction

Water has always captured man's attention, possibly because it is so vital to life. Perhaps it is natural that man should try to recreate, in

The Chinese not only introduced the concept of the garden pond, but they also developed colorful varieties of wild fish to be kept in them.

miniature, aquatic scenes. Since as far back as the ancient Chinese dynasties, people have had a high regard for ornamental ponds in their gardens. Here they could sit in solitude to contemplate life.

The Japanese were also keen on water gardens. They were, and still are, superb breeders of fish.

Other civilizations as well placed great emphasis on the peaceful nature of a water garden. Both the early Indian

and Arabic cultures featured exotic displays of water within their palaces and great homes. Simple, geometric lines were utilized in the Arabic constructions. Possibly the finest remaining example of Arabic ponds are found in the Moorish palace of the Alhambra in Granada, Spain. There, in the palace gardens, are many pools, fountains and ponds banked by cypress, rose, oleander, and myrtle.

The garden pool became a popular feature somewhat later in the more northerly European countries. The early Romans, renowned for their ingenuity with water for baths and viaducts, featured simple ponds within their designs. By the 18th century, ponds and lavishly designed fountains were fashionable with the nobility. No palace or large home was complete without at least one major pond installation. The gardens at Tivoli in Rome, the magnificent fountains and ponds of the Versailles palace in France, and the superb classic English gardens are all testimony to the role of water, fish, and plants in various civilizations throughout history.

Not until the 20th century could the average person consider featuring a pond in the

A garden pond in springtime. The design of your pond will be largely influenced by the amount of space that is available.

3

home. This was because the cost of the material and the problems of keeping the water clear were beyond the capabilities of most people. This situation has changed dramatically over the last 20 years. Today's population earns more, has more leisure time, and the technology of maintaining fish and water has made great advances.

Possibly because the weather in Europe was not favorable for a swimming pool, the garden pond was an established hobby before it caught on in the United States. Now, Americans too are developing ponds in large numbers. All this popularity is good for pond owners because it means a better range of equipment at more affordable prices.

A large yard or garden is not necessary for the construction of a pond. A small one may be accommodated in an apartment, a basement or on a patio or balcony. Even a collapsible swimming pool can be transformed into an attractive pond.

There is a lot more to the hobby than just the pond itself. Plants, fish, fountains, and other decorations allow for a great deal of challenge and creativity. The water must be monitored regularly to provide a balanced ecosystem to support the fish and plant life. A well-maintained pond is a great place to relax, unwind, and relieve the stress of daily life.

If you are unable to have an outdoor garden pond, e.g., if you lack the space, you might consider an indoor arrangement. With careful planning, your pond set-up can be as attractive as the one shown here.

Pre-construction Considerations

Do not install a pond without thoughtful and careful consideration first. Every aspect must be planned, and ample leeway must be allowed for any later needs. Oftentimes things do not work out precisely as planned. Therefore, the more thought you put into making decisions, the less chance there is that problems will develop later on.

at the lowest point in the garden to equate the situation of natural pools. However, you may prefer a different spot.

SITING

Probably the most fundamental decision to be made is where to site the pond. It is at this stage that the first problems can be encountered; therefore a degree of compromise may be necessary. Ideally, a pond should be placed

An interesting effect can be created by using the soil taken out for the pond. The dirt can be built up into the rockery behind the pool. This is a nice backdrop feature, and useful as well. It can house things such as pumps and filter systems.

Designing the layout of your garden pond can be a satisfying creative endeavor.

Do your best to site the pond away from trees. Trees send out powerful roots to search for water and the roots of nearby trees will eventually reach a pond and penetrate it. The resulting loss of water is a problem not easily rectified.

Overhanging branches block out a lot of sunlight. Garden ponds require light for healthy fish and plant growth. Additionally, deciduous trees shed their leaves in the fall. Dead leaves in a pond are unsightly and poisonous; in addition, they give off toxic chemicals which harm both the fish and plants. More unwanted debris and deadly gases are created as the leaves sink and rot.

Trees are hosts to many forms of animal life. Insects and birds may be dangerous to the fish, and they can also pollute the water with feces. For all these reasons, the pond should be located away from trees. However, a screen of conifers may help maintain a more even water temperature by providing a windbreak from cold northerly winds.

The distance from your home to the pond is also of importance. It is nice to be able to look at the pool from the comfort of your home. This way the pond can be enjoyed even on cold or windy days. Furthermore, the closer to your home the pond is, the easier and cheaper it is to get water and electricity to it.

SHAPE AND SIZE

Generally, if your garden is neatly laid out with flower borders in straight, geometric patterns, then a formal pool with similar lines is preferred. A formal pond is the choice if you plan to feature fountains and ornaments. An informal pool with more natural curves and an apparent lack of planning is at its best in a rambling, non-symmetrical garden. Plants and waterfalls

are better suited to an informal pond.

Of course, the amount of space and money you can devote to building a pond are important factors in determining pond size. A large pond is actually easier to maintain than is a small one. It also supports more fish and plants. However, its initial cost is higher and more hours are needed for its construction.

Permission from your local planning board may be required before you install the pond. This is an important consideration to check out. Also, be sure that no sewer lines or electrical cables run under the proposed site.

With good planning, even the smallest of garden ponds can be a beautiful creation.

All electrical apparatus near or in the water must be of the highest standard. Having it professionally installed is the best alternative for those pond builders who are not knowledgeable on the subject. The local authority may require detailed plans and an inspection. Large ponds, but not

usually small ones, may mean an increase in water and sewage charges from the local authority.

COSTS

Once you have an idea of the type and size of pond you desire, the cost of the construction can be estimated. This includes the cost of the materials from which the pool itself is made, as well as the accessories (such as pumps and filters) and labor. All these variables must be seriously considered until you arrive at an affordable and satisfactory figure. This may mean reducing the size of the pond or opting for a different construction material. It is far better to have a small pool that functions correctly than a large pool with an inadequate filter system.

Some pond builders would like to finish the project as quickly as possible. It is often better to make the construction a long-term project, though. In this way, you can have exactly the layout you want without compromising the quality of the equipment. Remember that a garden pond is a permanent feature. Once it is built, it is difficult to modify or

remove, so be sure it is developed to your taste and satisfaction during the construction.

One idea is to build a very small pond with the plan that it will be part of a larger connecting unit in the future. Valuable experience can be garnered in this fashion which can be used later on when you build the main pool.

View as many set-ups as possible before embarking on this venture. Visit friends who own ponds, garden centers, and public water gardens. Study books with pictures of garden ponds. Many ideas can be picked up from these sources. Discuss pumps and filters with specialists to be sure you select the equipment you need to clean and drive the volume of water in your pool. Good planning prevents future problems.

Constructing a pond used to be a long and tiresome procedure. The range of materials available today enables you to install a small, simple pond in very little time.

Fountains add another dimension to a garden pond. This simple but elegant pond design complements the surrounding landscape.

9

Even building a concrete pond is easier because of mini-sized mixers that can be rented.

There are several materials that can be used to build a pond. These are pond liners, prefabricated ponds, and concrete. The advantages and drawbacks of each will be discussed so that you can choose the material best suited to your ideas.

POND LINERS

Liners are sheets of waterproof material. Once water is poured into them, they take the shape of any hole into which they are placed. Liners come in three types.

Polyethylene liners are the least expensive type. They are available in a number of sizes. There are two main disadvantages to them, however. First, they rarely last more than two or three years before leakage occurs. Second, because they are thin, the liners are easily damaged when being installed. So polyethylene is not the recommended material of choice for a liner.

PVC, or polyvinyl chloride, is available in an assortment of colors and sizes. It is thicker than polyethylene, and so has a longer lifespan. It is also less affected by ultra-violet rays which create a slow decomposition of the liners. Since PVC is not as pliable as other liners, it does not always fit the contours of the pond as snugly. A little more effort is required in trying to smooth out the wrinkles.

Rubber compound liners are the most expensive, but they are also the best. They combine long life with excellent molding features due to their elasticity. They are more resistant to tearing as well.

Calculating the liner size is relatively simple. The equation is length + twice the depth x width + twice the depth, + an extra yard on length and width to allow for overlap around the edges. A simple rectangular pond of 4 yds x 3 yds with a depth of 1 yd requires 42 square yards of liner. When laid out on the lawn, this looks far larger than the size of the pond!

If you prefer an unusually-shaped pool, take the maximum dimensions of the length and width and calculate as stated. If the pond has varying depths, be on the safe side, use the deepest part of the pond in the equation. If you intend to have connecting

pools, treat them as two units rather than calculating for a single sheet of liner. There may be enough liner material remaining to connect the two pools with waterproof silicone rubber bonding glue.

The rhythmical cascades of a waterfall enhance the overall appeal of a pond.

When planning the interior of your garden pond, consider the needs of the plants that you have selected. It is better to have a modest collection of sturdy, flourishing plants rather than profuse plantings that are overcrowded and in poor condition.

PREFABRICATED PONDS

Ready-made ponds come in a range of sizes, shapes, and qualities. Such ponds merely require digging a hole, placing them in the ground and filling them up with water.

Vacuum-formed pools are at the inexpensive end of the scale. They are light in weight, but flexible and brittle. They have to be installed with great care and special attention must be given to their weakest stress points (usually where the depth changes).

Fiberglass pools are tougher, heavier, and more expensive. Give special consideration to the depth of the pond and the width of the shelves. Some pools are much too shallow; the fish will become too hot in the summer and may freeze in the winter. Likewise, plants need at least 13cm (5 in) of depth. If

you plan to place potted plants in the deeper water, the base area must be large enough to accommodate them. A pond may look large in the garden center, but once in the ground it "shrinks" considerably in size.

CONCRETE PONDS

A concrete or concrete-lined brick pond is the most permanent. Fewer are seen today than in the past. A concrete pond has strength, long-life, and can be fashioned into any shape. The major drawback is the effort required to construct it. However, a concrete pool decorated with tiles or stonework can be quite a showpiece.

The availability of butyl rubber and fiberglass allows a pond builder to achieve comparable size and durability with far less work.

Construction

Having selected the site and the type of garden pond, now it's time for the installation. While preparing the pond, don't forget about fitting the filter system, bottom drains, dry wells, water pipes, electrical cables, and water and outlet pipes. The extent of each of these is governed by the overall size of the pond itself.

MARKING THE SITE

Mark out the site with a garden hose. In the case of concrete ponds, an area larger than the actual pool must be marked to allow for the thickness of the walls. Next, the soil is removed. A good spade and a pick are required.

SHAPING THE POND

Up to now, the external shape of the pond has been considered. Some thought must also be given to the internal shape.

If the pond is to contain fish the whole year 'round, it should have at least one good-sized area of deep water. This serves two purposes. First, the fish need deep water in which to spend their inactive winter rest period. Second, they need deep water, during periods of hot weather, to provide a cool retreat. Shallow ponds freeze more quickly and their temperature fluctuates more drastically than deep ponds. The deepest point of the pond should be about 1.18 m (4 ft). If it can be deeper, that's even better. Vertical side walls also help to maintain a more stable

temperature, but most ponds feature sloping walls. You could have both types of walls in one pond.

Bear in mind that neither the depth nor the volume of the water determines the number of fish that can be kept. Rather, it

is the surface area that is of prime importance.

Marginal plants require shallow water, as do spawning fish. Therefore, a number of shelves of varying depths should be included in the design. The shelves should be of sufficient width, at least 15cm (6 in), to accommodate plants in baskets.

Once the shape has been fashioned, check that it is level in all areas. Otherwise, you may have a pool that brims at one end. Remove from the soil any sharp objects that might pierce the liner. Remember that the pond water will exert a tremendous force on the liner.

After you have packed and smoothed the contours, an extra layer of sand can be added to

cushion the liner. Add an inch to the base and the shelves. The side walls can be coated with water-soaked cardboard or paper so the sand will stick to it.

Now the site is ready for the liner. The liner should be laid on the ground for an hour in the sunshine. This heat treatment will improve its elasticity a bit.

Polyethylene liners are fitted in a manner different from the others. The liner is placed in the pond. Then, starting at the deepest point and working toward the sides, it is pressed into position. A little slack is allowed so that there is

The completed pond. Now comes the most enjoyable part of your project: the addition of plants and/or fish.

The beautiful end result.

15

some allowance for flexibility as the water is added. No stress should be placed on any one point.

Next, water is added via a hose placed in the deep end. As many wrinkles as possible should be ironed out as the pond fills. Excess edging is trimmed when the pond is full. Sufficient edging must be left to be weighted down by the paving that completes the installation. If you are going to use slabs as a border, remove enough soil around the pond edge so that the slabs are flush with the lawn.

PVC and butyl rubber liners are fitted by being stretched over the pond and weighted down with bricks or slabs. Next, water is hosed into the center of the liner. Slowly the weight of the water presses the liner into the pond. The side weights are eased in stages as the pond fills. Once full, the excess liner is trimmed and slabs fitted to complete the job.

A fiberglass pond requires a rectangular excavation site into which the pond will fit. The site should be slightly deeper than the maximum depth of the

to check that the pond is level.

Edging slabs should rest neatly over the edge of the pool. The slabs require only a small overhang. Too much overhang may result in the fish being injured by jumping into the slabs.

It may be useful to attach waterproof tape around the top edge of the liner, particularly a polyethylene liner that is exposed to direct sunlight. Such protection will prolong the life of the liner. Marginal plants will also help to screen exposed liner edges.

CONCRETE PONDS

Preparing a concrete pond is a time-consuming job. It should be attempted only when the hours

pond. This is because as earth is packed into the sides, the pond will be raised up slightly—and you do not want the pool to be higher than the surrounding ground. Making the hole a bit larger leaves plenty of room for backfill. Pack the earth well into the sides, making sure that it is even.

Place a couple of inches of loose soil or sand in the base. This allows the pond to settle as the water is added, without undue stress at a particular point. Keep a spirit level handy

Statues and other decorative ornaments can be placed strategically to accent a particular area of the pond.

The actual arrangement of your pond and its contents is limited only by your imagination.

17

of daylight are long and the temperature is more conducive to setting the concrete. Late spring is a good time, before the days become too hot.

The thickness of a concrete pond should be at least 15.5cm (6 in) so it can withstand the seasonal changes in weather. The initial preparation in fashioning the shape is the same as for liner ponds. But remember that the excavation site must be enlarged 15.5cm (6 in) for the concrete walls and base.

Next comes the concrete. It can be mixed on the site or purchased ready-mixed. If the pond is well into your yard, mixing on the site is a better choice. Otherwise, you will

have a huge pile of concrete deposited in your driveway that must be hauled to the site, as well as a mess left on the driveway. Also, the operation will have to be completed before the concrete sets. Fortunately, mini-mixers can be rented which reduce a lot of the hard work.

The concrete mix should be one part cement, two parts sand and four parts gravel. The concrete must be mixed until its consistency is neither thick nor runny. It is possible to add waterproofing agents and dyes at the mixing stage.

A wooden framework, or shuttering, may be needed for the sides if the slope is steep or vertical. This woodwork should be hosed with water so that the concrete does not stick to it. The concrete can be laid to about two-thirds of the desired thickness. At this stage it may be beneficial to lay a screen of wire-mesh to act as a strengthener. Then the final third of the concrete can be added and smoothed over with a wet plastering trowel.

When laying concrete, ensure that it is well-rammed, especially if framework is used. If air pockets are allowed to remain, they may result in the concrete's flaking at a later date.

The size of the pond determines whether or not the project can be completed in one day. It is best to pour the entire pond at once. If this is not possible, though, score the surface and cover the pond overnight. Return to the job the next day or cracks will appear.

Once the concrete has been laid, it should be covered with wet sacking or lightly sprayed periodically if the weather is hot. Keeping the surface damp allows the concrete to set slowly. The result is stronger concrete.

Once the pond is completely hardened, the lime content must be reduced. This is an important step because without it, the water will be much too alkaline for the fish and plants. Two methods of reduction are

To prevent drainage problems, the location of your garden pond should be on ground that is level.

possible. First, the pond can be left empty for a few months. The elements will bleach out the lime. Or, the pond can be filled with water, emptied and scrubbed several times.

After reducing the lime content, a cement sealant should be used to lock in any lime still left. If a coloring agent was not added at the mixing stage, the pond can be painted the color of your choice. Be sure to use the manufacturer's recommended primer or the paint will not adhere to the concrete. A sealant can be applied on top of the paint if you desire. Given the low cost of polyethylene, it may be worthwhile to fit a lining to the pond as a backup against leaks.

CONCRETE CLAD BRICKWORK

You may be planning a pond partly above ground level with walls of brick. In such a case, the concrete rendering can be thinner, about 5cm (2 in). Use waterproof mortar and be sure the bricks are *soaked* with water before applying the concrete. Dry bricks will absorb the water from the concrete, resulting in a brittle finish prone to cracking.

Once the pond is complete, many owners promptly add both fish and plants. It is really sound policy to introduce the plants first. They act as a gauge of the suitability of the water; problems with the water will show themselves in poor plant growth. The water should be tested periodically and allowed to mature to the proper conditions for fish. This time can also be used for testing and adjusting the pond equipment. Adding the fish at a later date protects them from exposure to all this stress.

Your garden pond can be as simple or as elaborate as you desire.

Pumps and Filters

Fish produce nitrites and carbon dioxide as waste products. Plants utilize these materials, together with sunlight, to produce oxygen, and fish need oxygen to live. Thus, a balance should be achieved in your garden pond in which all inhabitants can live in harmony. When debris and harmful chemicals are in excess, this ecosystem is adversely affected; stagnation and deterioration are the result. To maintain a healthy balance, the pond must be fitted with pumps and filters which clean and revitalize the water.

FILTRATION

A filter system continually removes unwanted particles

Pond filtration equipment can be housed in a unit such as this.

which are suspended and dissolved in the water. This cleansing action creates an environment which is relatively stable. The fish and plants are protected from great fluctuations in the water condition, which can create stress.

There are three basic filtration systems: mechanical, chemical, and biological. One or a combination can be used in your pond. Filter systems can be either internal or external to the pond. Both types of systems pump water through the medium, aerate it, and then return it to the pond.

A small pond typically has an internal system that draws water in through slots, passes it through the filter medium, and then pumps it back to the pond via a pump within the filter unit. The currents produced can cause damage to some plants; therefore locate such filters away from delicate plants that do not like moving water.

Most filter systems pump water up through the filter medium. The water then exits from the top of the tank. This procedure can be reversed, though. Water can be pumped into the filter box and up a pipe so that it exits via the top of the pipe. It then travels down the filter medium and is returned to the pond via gravity. It could tumble from a waterfall or fountain as it enters the pond. This creates a pleasant effect as well as aerating the water.

There are a variety of filtration systems available. Have a good look around and talk with some experts about the merits of each.

An initial settling tank, which will trap the heaviest objects before allowing the water to pass through the filter, is advised. The most typical set-up is a drain fitted at the base of the pond. The floor area must slope to the drain. Several of these may be required in a large pond.

Drains can be bought or constructed by you. Commercial drains vary, depending on whether they are to be fitted to a concrete base or a liner. They contain a chamber or sump into which the dirt and water fall. From here a pipe carries the water to a holding tank with the water surface at

Most garden ponds will require a certain amount of mechanical support.

the same level as the pond. This way the water will rise, due to the pond water pressure, into the tank. A second pipe takes the dirty water to a dry well or into your home drainage system. Here a covering sleeve on the input pipe is removed. This sleeve is at a level higher than the pond water so that it acts effectively as a tap. (If your pond is at a high point, the outlet pipe can be operated by a valve which periodically releases the water to eliminate the need for a holding tank.)

If you do not install a drain, the accumulated mulm in the pond can be vacuumed out. Alternatively, the debris can be siphoned off if the pond is small and at a higher level than the receiving container for the dirty water.

Depending on the distance between the water surface and the surrounding ground, it may be necessary to incorporate an overflow pipe into the system. Average rainfall usually replaces water lost by evaporation, but heavy downpours may result in flooding. An overflow pipe, about 5cm (2 in) in diameter situated above the water surface and below ground level, will prevent this flooding. If your pond is above ground level, stand a pipe upright in the pond with its top just above the surface. Overflow then goes down this pipe to exit to a lower ground level. (This type of pipe must be incorporated in the design stage.) Whichever overflow pipe design you use, cover the pipe opening with fine mesh to prevent fish from being swept away.

FILTERS

Mechanical filtration removes solid objects from the water by acting as a strainer. The filter material allows water to pass through it, but it restricts solid particles. Materials such as sand, gravel, and charcoal are commonly used. Charcoal has dual functions: it acts as a mechanical filter as well as absorbing or converting harmful chemicals into other compounds. Quite often two or more filter mediums are used together. Owners of large ponds may have several tanks containing different mediums. The water is passed through ever finer filter material.

Biological filtration converts harmful chemicals to other compounds which can be used by the pond plants. One of the most toxic chemicals is the nitrogen compound ammonia. This is produced by the decomposition of proteins and feces, as well as by anaerobic bacteria which convert nitrates to ammonia. Since ammonia is water-soluble, it cannot be seen in the pond. It is converted into nitrates by aerobic bacteria. Nitrates are used by plants for growth. Aerobic bacteria can be encouraged to multiply by providing them a suitable medium. Gravel and well-oxygenated water are such mediums.

An under-gravel filter keeps a pond rich in oxygen. Such a filter is usually made of metal. It can be either a plate type, a series of plates or lengths of corrugated plastic. The filter should have a series of holes and be placed under a layer of gravel, pebbles or another suitable material. The filter must also have a tube going from it to the top of the pond.

An air supply is introduced into the tube from a pump. An airstone is fitted at the other end of the tube. As water travels through the gravel, it is purified by the bacteria. The water then returns to the surface via the airlift created by the airstone. In effect, a current of water is passing down from the upper levels and then back up by way of the airlift. A powerhead attached to the filter will improve performance because the rate of the water passing through the under-gravel filter is increased.

A series of pipes can be connected to a pick-up tube. In this way, a pump can draw water through the holes in the

It is important that the pumps you use are of adequate capacity. Special pond features such as waterfalls, which are powered by pumps, require special attention.

piping, through a mechanical filter and then back to the pond. In a reverse flow filtration situation, the filtered water is returned via the airlift tube. The water exits under the filter and rises through it, thus reversing the normal flow situation. However, this requires powerful pumps, and the water is not as placed in the deepest water. An extra 15.5cm (6 in) or so in depth is required for home-built ponds. This allows for the depth of the filter and the layer of gravel.

PUMPS

A pump circulates the water through the filter system. It also

The pattern of water spray is determined by the design of the fountain's spray head. Some hobbyists prefer a single spray of water whereas others prefer that the water sprays out in a fan-like fashion.

well-oxygenated as in a normal flow situation.

An undergravel system needs to take up about one-third of the pond's overall area. It should be improves the oxygen content of the pool by creating turbulence, which increases the actual surface area of the water. The turbulence has a secondary

The sides of the waterfall should extend beyond the actual water course so that the cascading water makes its way into the pond and doesn't flood the adjacent area.

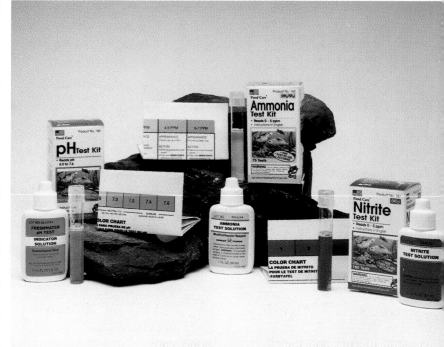

benefit as well; it helps to keep the pond at a more stable temperature throughout its depth.

Pumps may be placed away from the pond or submersed within it. The better ones have controls which govern the output rate. Smaller or inexpensive models may require clamps to restrict their output.

The size and number of pumps required is determined by the size of the pond. Therefore, when purchasing a pump, you must know its capacity of flow. This is expressed in the number of gallons pumped per hour (gph). Pumps for an average garden pond are sold in many pet stores. If your pond is large, you may need to contact a specialist water garden center that stocks high-flow-rate models.

Ideally, a pump should send the total volume of water contained in the pond through the filtration system in about one hour. (The water does not need to be circulated as quickly during the winter months because the fish are inactive at this time.) In calculating the pump size, include the water capacity of the filtration tanks. Since fountains and waterfalls consume a great deal of water, pumps in these situations need considerable capacities. It is better to have pumps working well within their capacities than pumps working at their limits.

WATER

The water in the garden pond must meet certain requirements vital for the proper functioning of the fish and plants. These criteria include the oxygen content, the pH and the hardness of the water.

The pond water must be tested at regular intervals in order that a proper ecosystem is maintained. There is more to good pond management than just filling up a pond with water and releasing fish into it. Good water conditions are as vital to fish and aquatic plants as good air is to humans. The cleaner and more suitable the water conditions are for the pond inhabitants, the healthier they will be, and the more pleasure you will get from your pond. Common sense is probably the most important aspect of good pond care.

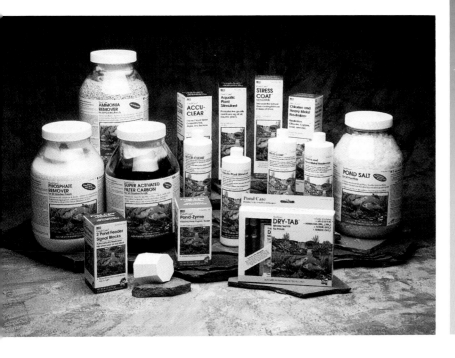

Many fine products are available for conditioning and treating the water in a pond—very important considerations in the health of the pond's inhabitants. Photo courtesy of Aquarium Pharmaceuticals.

AERATION

Coldwater fish require well-oxygenated water. During hot weather, the oxygen content of the pond reduces inversely as the temperature rises. Thus supplementary air is beneficial to the well-being of the fish.

The more surface area of water exposed to the air, the more oxygenated is the water. If water is allowed to hit the pond surface, the surface area of the pond is increased, thus providing for greater oxygenation. Spray bars can be fitted to the outlet pipes returning water to the pond from the filter, as well as to the hose that refills the pond. The fine spray thus created has much the same effect as a fountain.

Another variation is to fit a venturi to the filtration system. (A venturi is a nozzle-shaped accessory that attaches to the pump pipe.) Here, the water from the pump meets a restriction along its length. Just beyond the restriction is an air intake. A partial vacuum is created which sucks air into the water. Air can be brought in via a short tube near the pond.

Alternatively, the oxygen content can be raised by using an airstone placed next to a tube into which air is pumped. The amount of dissolved oxygen produced is determined by the number and size of the bubbles and the time it takes the bubbles to burst before reaching the surface. The smaller the bubbles, the more likely that air will enter the water. Placing the airstone in the deepest part of the pond increases the time it takes for the bubbles to reach the surface.

pH

The pH of water is described as acidic, neutral or alkaline, depending upon the amount of hydrogen ions it contains. The higher the content of hydrogen ions, the more acidic the water.

The pH value is measured on a logarithmic scale of 0 to 14. At 0, the water is acid; at 14, it is alkaline. A reading of 7 is neutral. Most freshwater fish prefer a reading between 6.5 and 7.5. Hence, the fish are quite adaptable.

You may think that a variation of just one point is hardly adaptable. But remember, the pH scale is logarithmic. This means that water with a reading of 7.5 is ten times more alkaline than water with a reading of 6.5!

A test kit purchased from your local dealer permits you to easily check the pH value. Many types of kits are on the market. All of them compare a water sample with a graduated color chart to indicate the value.

The pH value must be checked on a regular basis. Problems are unlikely if you have a good filter system, though. Adding peat to the filter medium will lower the pH, while adding limestone or chalk will raise it.

HARDNESS

Water with a high content of dissolved salt is referred to as hard. Soft water has a low level of dissolved salt. Essentially, hardness can be checked by the use of a test kit. It can be corrected by boiling water, which reduces the hardness, and then cooling it before adding it to the pond. Adding sodium bicarbonate has the same effect.

Or, manufactured resins can be added to the filter system.

NITRITES

A specialized test kit to determine the nitrite levels in the pond can be bought. This is particularly useful if your pond does not have a biological filter, or if the colony of bacteria is not yet built up enough to cope with the amount of ammonia in the water.

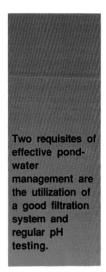

Two requisites of effective pond-water management are the utilization of a good filtration system and regular pH testing.

Fountains and Waterfalls

Extra features, such as fountains and waterfalls, add that something special to a garden pond. The assortment from which you can choose is enormous, from small plastic or fiberglass ornaments to grand dolphins, shells, and mermaids of concrete or metal. A fountain can be simple, or it can be a complex unit spraying patterns illuminated by colored lenses. A waterfall can be a small flow of water dripping over rocks, or you may prefer an elaborate staircase effect. Indeed, a real enthusiast can have the entire lighting and pumping system controlled by timer switches.

PUMPS

A few points about pumps should be noted in regard to fountains and waterfalls. A submersible pump is suitable if only a single fountain is planned. In this type of set-up, water is sent from the pump to a tube. The spray head is either fixed or variable to allow the water flow rate and the spray

Some pond-keepers choose to make the waterfall the main focus of their pond. Others prefer to supplement the visual appeal of the waterfall with plants and decorative objects.

pattern to be changed. Altering the spray pattern is a matter of changing a spray disc. The height of the spray is controlled both by the size of the holes in the disc and the pressure of the water.

If one pump serves a number of accessories, be sure it has sufficient water capacity. Even a modest waterfall can require 250 gallons per hour to achieve the desired effect. So if a fountain is utilized as well, you will probably need a pump with about a 500-600 gallon capacity. Of course, filtered water can be returned via waterfalls and fountains. You may prefer that the filter be separate from the displays, though. In such a case, a "T"

junction and valves, situated near the pond end of the filtered water, allow you to cut off the fountain when required.

If your pump has only a short electrical cable attached via a connector cable to the main power supply, have the extension placed discreetly under a slab not too far from the pond. Then the pump can be disconnected for servicing or during the winter months. A heater unit can be hooked up during cold weather if you desire. This arrangement prevents having lots of cable on each electrical unit.

A surface pump must be

housed in dry conditions where it can be serviced easily, such as in a mini-pump house. Also, if the pump is at a greater height than the pond, it should be positioned so that the height between the water and the pump is shorter than the height between the pump and the head. The head is the exit point of the pumped water.

A valve is necessary to retain the prime, which is the water in the pipe between the pond and the pump. If the pump is at a level lower than the pond, the prime will not need a valve because it will be maintained by the force of gravity. It is always wise to have the pipes going to fountains or waterfalls in the straightest, shortest route, thus placing less strain on the pump.

A pump is an important part of your garden pond. An investment in a quality model is money well spent. Ideally, a pump should be able to work continually and be trouble-free for a long while. Be sure that the service and spare parts are readily available. It is best to

Ideally, your pond should have enough of a border so that you can walk all around it. This will permit easy access for pond maintenance.

deal with a well-established manufacturer that specializes in water garden equipment.

FOUNTAINS

The lighting units and adapters used for a fountain must be designed for aquatic use. Besides the lighting that is actually in the pond, a good effect can be achieved by the strategic use of colored spotlights on the pond edge or hidden in vegetation near the pond.

The type of spray head fitted to the fountain is important to obtain the best nighttime effect. If possible, the water should fall over the lighting as a single sheet.

Some varieties of plants, such as water lilies, should not be placed near fountains. Such plants prefer slow-moving water and smooth water surfaces. One way to slow the movement of the water from a fountain is to have the water spill into a receptacle instead of hitting the pond surface directly. A number of these spillover situations can be devised. The receiving bowls must be level; otherwise the water will not tumble over the side evenly, which is the best visual effect.

WATERFALLS

A waterfall adds a nice touch to a garden pond. It has a natural look about it and can provide a backdrop for a rock garden.

The width of the waterfall is governed by the capacity of the pump. This is because the key to a successful waterfall lies in the volume of water passing over it. The sides of the waterfall must be somewhat raised so they are at a higher level than the water passing over them. Otherwise, your rockery will be flooded.

The sight and sound of a waterfall create a setting that is both beautiful and serene.

A watercourse must be prepared, just as was done with the pond. The watercourse can be made from a liner, fiberglass, or concrete. Fiberglass units can be purchased which fit into one another, enabling you to devise a variety of combinations. Liners can be fashioned into more flexible shapes, but it can be difficult to make something intricate.

Concrete is best if you want a twisting path with falls at differing heights.

Give the various steps of the watercourse a slightly backward slope. Then, when the pump is turned off, some water will be retained at each level.

Rocks can be placed down the watercourse and suitable plants, such as ferns, added near the water's edge. A terrace of granite slabs can be built at the last fall for the water to cascade over. The last fall should have its edge extended slightly so that all the water goes into the pond and not onto the pond edge. If you don't want the water from each level merely to trickle down the face of the fall, have a small edge extend beyond each level. Everything really depends on the effect you want to create.

A staircase waterfall can be achieved by cementing sewer or plastic pipes above and just behind the other. The wider the pipe, the greater the amount of water necessary to get the desired look.

Aquatic Plants

Plants, fish, and ponds are a natural combination. Some pond owners, though, cultivate only plants, while others devote their time only to fish. Most pond owners create a balanced ecosystem containing both fish and plants.

A selection of plants, including weeds and wild grasses, that grow naturally in your area is a good choice. They are well-suited to your soil and are prolific without requiring special attention. Choose those with varying periods of flowering so that there are plants in full bloom as much of the year as possible.

When selecting aquatic plants, choose those that are suited to the climatic conditions of the area in which you live.

Consider the size of the plant in relation to the size of the pond. Do not choose one so large that it will overwhelm a small pond. Do not place a tall one where it may obscure some other attractive pond feature.

Bear in mind that many species of plants prefer slow-moving water. Therefore, the more rigorous your filter system, the fewer plants can the pond support. The water flow must be adjusted to create the balance acceptable to their particular need.

PLANT TYPES

Aquatic plants can be divided into one of four broad groups. First, there are those which flower above the water and have a fixed root system. Marginal plants may be included in this group. Second, there are those which are free-floating; their roots act as stabilizers and draw nutrients from the water. Third, there are submerged plants. Fourth, there are the bog plants. These are at their best in very damp situations.

PLANTING MEDIA

Other than free-floaters, all plants require a suitable medium in which to grow. The most popular is garden soil that has been well-sifted. Loam, a mixture of sand and clay, is another good choice for water plants.

The planting medium can be placed directly onto the pond base and shelves. However, it is better to put the marginal plants into baskets. Thus you can remove the basket from the water if the plant requires pruning or winter storage. Submerged plants can be planted in the bottom media, or they can be placed in containers.

Some pond-keepers prefer an abundant growth of plants, with few fish; others prefer just the opposite arrangement. How your pond is stocked is up to you.

A layer of gravel should be placed over the planting medium. This keeps the medium in place and prevents the fish from disturbing the plant roots. It also acts as a biological filter.

Those plants requiring a winter rest period may be transferred either to indoor tanks or wintered in an appropriate substrate in a dry state. The old leaves and roots should be pruned. When returning young plants to the pond, weight the roots with ceramic balls. These are better to use than lead weights.

PURCHASING PLANTS

Most popular submersible plants are readily available in pet or aquatic stores, because the same species of plants are used in tropical and coldwater fish tanks. Taller marginal plants may require a visit to a garden center.

Select only young, healthy-looking plants. Be sure any one you choose is suitable for a garden pond and that it prefers the conditions (pH, hardness) found in your pond. Remove any dead or dying leaves.

If you think a plant has been sprayed with an insecticide or other chemical, pass it over. Likewise, avoid using pesticides and similar products anywhere near your garden pond. These chemicals can be lethal to both fish and aquatic plants.

When selecting plants for your pond, bear in mind that the foliage and the roots (if not contained in a pot) will spread out; therefore make due allowance for this growth when siting the plants.

Plants normally fare better if they are placed in groups of their own species. This prevents the more robust types from overpowering the more delicate species. Remember, too, a good display of fewer varieties is more pleasing to the eye than an abundance of varieties in sparse groups.

FLOWERING PLANTS

The water lily is the most notable flowering plant for a garden pond. There is an exciting range from which to choose, including dwarf species which can be grown in as little as 15.5cm (6 in) of water, to larger species which can thrive in depths of 1m (3 ft 3 in). Lilies look superb, and their spreading leaves provide cool areas of shade for the fish and retard the growth of algae. They like lots of sunshine and water that is neutral to slightly acid; they do not like turbulent water. Keep them away from filter exit pipes, fountains, and waterfalls.

Lilies should be planted in the spring. They should be placed in a basket so that just the tip is above the soil and gravel. Put them in shallow water at first. Once the rootstock is established, they can be placed in deeper water.

Lilies hibernate in the winter. The old leaves must be pruned, and the plants stored in either a dry state or damp soil. Those not lifted from the water will be less vigorous.

Lilies come in a wealth of flower colors. The common white water lily is *Nymphaea alba*. Red is *N. rubra*. Blue is available in the *N. micrantha*,

The water hyacinth and other species of the genus *Eichhornia* are noted for their distinctive, colorful blossoms.

stellata and *coeruela.* Yellow is seen in *N. dentata, sulfurea* and *marliacea.* The list of species and their hybrids is enormous.

Within the Nymphaeceae family are other attractive and less expensive lily-like plants. *Brasenia schreberi* is suitable for shallow waters. The leaves have green centers and a reddish tinge to the edges. The flowers are a reddish-purple.

A pretty lily-like plant for deeper pond areas is *Nuphar lutea.* It has green, heart-shaped leaves and golden-yellow flowers. This species is commonly called "brandy bottle" due to its alcoholic fragrance.

Flowers of the family Iridaceae, which contains the crocus and gladiola, are popular with gardeners. Pond owners are most interested in the genus *Iris.* These are tall flowers of the shallows or the bog garden. The violet-blue species includes *I. laevigata.* It may attain a height of 75cm (30 in). A smaller species, *I. spuria,* reaches only 60cm (24 in). *I. versicolor* may grow to over 100cm (39 in). Yellow is seen in *I. pseudocorus,* which reaches heights of 150cm (50 in). Yellow comes in a variety

Another popular floating plant is the water soldier, *Stratiotes aloides.*

of shades, deepening almost to orange.

Pontederia cordata—pickerelweed—is a nice plant which grows to 75cm (30 in). It has a spike of flowers in violet-blue and wide, spear-shaped leaves. Grow this plant in shallow water with a maximum depth of 31cm (12 in), or in the bog ground near the pond.

For an exotic touch, try plants of the genus *Lysichitum*. They grow to 90cm (35 in). The white or yellow forms a sheath around a spiked, green spadix.

The genus *Hosta* is nice for its delicate, pendant, bell-like flowers. The flower colors range from lilac to pale blue. Twenty-five or more flowers may appear on the 75cm (30 in) stems. The green leaves are spear-shaped, edged with white, and form a dense mass of foliage.

A stand of reedmace (cattails, bulrushes) is commonplace, particularly in a large, informal pond. There are nine species in the family Typhaceae, all contained in the single genus *Typha*. Reeds grow from 45cm (18 in) to 243cm (8 ft) in height. The brown and white flowers on the tall, single stems make an attractive contrast against the bright colors of other plants. They are rampant growers.

Two interesting families of wild plants are Primulaceae, the primulas, and Ranunculaceae, which includes the marsh marigolds of the genus *Calthus*. These families provide a wealth of both tall and short flowered plants. Many have cultivated hybrids as well.

Various grass-like plants can be featured in and around a pond. These provide a soft, gentle, and natural touch to an

informal pond. Within the Cyperaceae and Gramineae families, there are some 12,000 species. Limit your selection to grasses of the genera *Cyperus* and *Carex*.

FLOATING PLANTS

Most floating species are actually anchored to the substrate. This section looks at the true free-floating plants. Floating plants offer refuge to fish fry, and many are included in the diet of fish, such as goldfish.

The water hyacinth *Eichhornia crassipes* and its related species are considered weeds in their South American habitat. The plant sports a beautiful blue flower during the summer months. Even the roots are an attractive bluish-black color. It is a delicate plant if

raised in temperate climates. Warm, humid conditions are necessary for it to be at its best. The water hyacinth may root in shallow water under 1m (3 ft 3 in).

The Hydrocharitaceae family contains plants of interest to both water gardeners and aquarists. The small, white-flowered frogbit, *Hydrocharis morsus-ranae*, is a hardy plant found in both Europe and Asia. Its leaves are heart-shaped. Another white-flowered plant from this family is the water soldier, *Stratiotes aloides*. Its blossoms are 3 to 4cm (1.25 in) in diameter. Both the frogbit and water soldier grow in slightly alkaline water.

The water chestnut, *Trapa natans*, is another member of this family with white flowers. Its leaves are rhomboid-shaped and have dentate margins to their top two edges.

A few pond plants quickly form blankets of green on the water surface. If kept in check, they make nice nibbling areas for fish. Pteridophytes, or ferns, are found in the genus *Salvinia*. These plants have small, round, oblong or oval leaves. They are often seen in association with water lilies.

Azolla caroliniana is another fern common to ponds. It has small clusters of scaly leaves. This plant and its related species do best in shallow water.

The liverworts also create a blanket cover. One of the most common is crystalwort, *Riccia fluitans*. It appears as undefined, string-like masses of green thallus; the plant body is not differentiated into stems, roots and leaves.

Duckweed, *Lemna minor*, has light green, round or oval leaves about 8mm (.33 in) in diameter. It must be monitored strictly or it will quickly take over the pond to the detriment of submerged plants. A related genus, *Wolffia*, is totally rootless.

Water lettuce, *Pistia stratiotes*, is lettuce-like in appearance. It does not like cold, rainy weather.

SUBMERGED PLANTS

The mainstream of plants popular in aquariums comes within this group. Submerged plants help to maintain healthy water by absorbing minerals and generating oxygen. They also create a balanced biosystem by providing refuge for numerous microscopic forms of animals.

The Hydrocharitaceae family includes *Vallisneria spiralis*, *Hydrilla lithuanica* and *Elodea canadensis*. Canadian pondweed, *E. canadensis*, is probably the most common submerged species. The plant can grow to heights of 3m (9.75 ft). It has paired, dark green

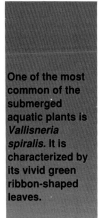

One of the most common of the submerged aquatic plants is *Vallisneria spiralis*. It is characterized by its vivid green ribbon-shaped leaves.

the movement of the water. A plant can be free-floating or a rhizome with whorls of leaves radiating from a single stem. These species encourage the growth of plankton, so they are good for browsing fish. All the species, except *M. alternifolium*, prefer hard and alkaline water with slow currents.

The family Nymphaeaceae contains a submerged plant, the *Cabomba*, which flowers like a lily. It has feather-like leaves radiating from the stems. It is a delicate plant which enjoys neutral to acid water.

Ceratophyllum submersum, the hornwort, is a soft, feather-type plant. It grows to a height of 1m (39 in). The stem may have one or two forks. It likes neutral water which is somewhat hard. A related species, *C. demersum*, is darker green.

The genus *Cryptocoryne* includes a number of plants which are interesting for their lanceolate leaves and their inflorescences (the flowering part of the stem above the last

leaves at its lower points which combine in whorls of three higher up the stem. This is a rampant grower. It prefers somewhat alkaline water. *E. densa*, with its whorls of four leaves, may be a better choice for ponds.

V. spiralis has tall, ribbon-like leaves. They emerge from a stolon in the substrate to create bunches. This species likes neutral to acidic water.

H. lithuanica has a slim stem from which whorls of three to five pale green leaves grow. The margins of the leaves are serrated at the tips. This plant is suited to the shallower areas, up to 1m (39 in), of a pond.

The water milfoil, *Myriophyllum* spp, is a nice choice if you like delicate, fern-like plants that gently sway with stem leaves). These plants are prone to leaf decomposition. They survive best in soft, neutral to acid water. They also like a slightly shaded area. The substrate should be river sand that is 10% peat. Keep these plants only if you live in a warm climate, have a glasshouse pond, or are able to winter the plants indoors.

C. beckettii, lutea and *nevillii* are some of the more hardy species of this genus. *C. beckettii* grows from rootstock that can be cut to contain a bud and a root which can be propagated in shallow water. The leaves are a brownish color. *C. lutea* sports green leaves. It has lanceolate-oval leaves growing on 15cm (6 in) stalks. *C. nevillii* is dark green. It has both short and long leaves. This is a good foreground plant that will spread to form a blanket of green. It likes a humus substrate.

The genus *Aponogeton* provides some magnificent plants for aquarists. *A. fenestralis* has lattice-like leaves. It is too delicate for an outdoor pond. Some other species, such as *A. distachyus*, can be utilized by the water gardener. It has elliptical leaves which initially are submerged, but then float. It sports a whitish, scented flower. This plant is suited to depths up to 45cm (18 in). It is commonly

Maintaining the proper water condition is essential to the health of the plants.

known as water hawthorn or Cape pondweed.

The genus *Potamogeton* has many plants that can cope with cold water. A number of species grow well in moving water. An example is *P. crispus*. It has long, wavy, slim leaves. They are brownish-red to green depending on the type of water and the extent of sunlight. The stems may be 120cm (48 in) long.

Another plant that survives in moving water is *Fontinalis antipyretica*, water moss. Its stems reach up to 50cm (24 in). Tufts of vegetation carry small, green, oval leaves. It likes neutral and medium hard water.

If you want to include a grass-like plant, try the spike bush, *Eleocharis acicularis*. It rarely grows beyond 30cm (12 in). Bunches of stems are formed from a runner.

Duckweed, *Lemna minor,* is a hardy and prolific plant. If it does not receive regular attention, it can be harmful to other plants in the pond.

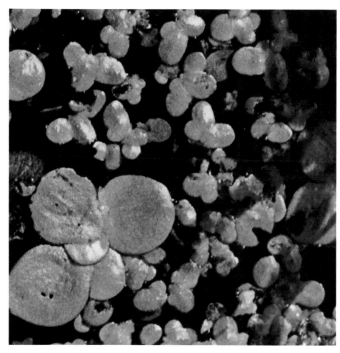

Fishes

The most common type of pondfish is goldfish. A more ambitious enthusiast may prefer magnificent koi. There are other species of fish suitable for pondlife. They may not be as glamorous in color, but they are useful to the pond ecosystem.

This chapter is merely an overview of some of the considerations involved when keeping pondfish. Consult a book about pondfish, goldfish, or koi for a more comprehensive discussion.

STOCKING CAPACITY

Fish breathe oxygen which is dissolved in the water. Therefore, the amount of dissolved oxygen in the water determines the number of fish that can be kept. The amount of oxygen in a volume of water is determined by the surface area; the depth is of no particular importance.

To calculate the stocking capacity of a given pond, the rule is that for every 25mm (1 in) of fish body (excluding the tail), allow 155 square centimeters (24 square inches) of water surface.

When calculating these figures, use the full adult size of the fish. If you use the size of immature fish, there will be no

The common goldfish, *Carassius auratus,* is the best choice of pond fish for the novice pond-keeper.

better to understock a pond than to stock it to capacity.

WATER VOLUME

It is useful to know the volume of water in the pond. You

allowance for growth. Also, as the temperature rises in the pond, the oxygen content is reduced. Therefore, it is far

need to know this when choosing a pump or if you introduce medicines into the pond. In many cases, a pond

may have shelves or varying levels of depth. In this instance, an average depth must be estimated. If the pond is a complex shape, work out the calculations as though the pond were a number of separate circles and regular shapes.

WATER DEPTH

If you live in more northerly climates where

temperatures fall below freezing, and you plan to accommodate fish over the winter, depth is an important consideration. The pond should be at least 91cm (36 in) deep for goldfish and 122cm (48 in) for koi. These depths ensure that

temperatures. The optimum temperature is about 17°C (63°F) during the summer, and about 4 °C (39°F) during the winter rest period.

SELECTING FISH

Purchase fish only from

the lower reaches of the pond do not freeze. It is here that the fish will spend their winter rest period.

TEMPERATURE

Both goldfish and koi can survive in a wide range of

clean, well-organized establishments. Good conditions help to maintain healthy fish. Avoid dealers with dirty or overcrowded tanks.

Select a fish that swims steadily and in a controlled manner. The scales should be

The fish that you select for your garden pond should be of top quality. Remember to quarantine new fish for about three weeks.

complete, with no signs of damage or parasites. All fins should be intact; no pieces should be torn or missing. The eyes and nostrils should be clear. Choose specimens that exhibit good color, particularly if you plan to breed the fish.

FEEDING

There are two basic rules to remember when feeding goldfish and koi. The first is to feed them a little at a time, about twice a day. The second is to provide as much of a variety as possible. Both

vegetables and animal protein should be given.

Fish are quite inactive during the winter, and the food intake drops proportionately. There should be minimal or no food offered at this time. Fish are most active during the summer. However, if you should go on vacation, pondfish can survive up to two weeks without being fed. They will live off their fat reserves and can nibble on the live plants.

When you purchase the fish, find out what they have been eating. Continue this diet,

Pet shops usually carry a wide range of foods for pond fishes and other pool inhabitants. Photo courtesy of Wardley.

This collection of koi illustrates the vivid splashes of color for which these fish are noted. Visually speaking, an overpopulated pond can lessen the viewer's appreciation of the subtleties in coloration.

gradually introducing a wider range of food.

INTRODUCING FISH TO THE POND

It is wise to isolate new fish for about three weeks. A fish that looks well may actually be incubating an illness. This

quarantine protects established fish from becoming infected with disease. Most ailments will show themselves in three weeks. Any diseased fish can be treated or destroyed.

When bringing a fish home, it will probably be in a plastic bag with a suitable amount of water. The bag should float for about an hour in the fish's new home. This allows the temperature of the water in the bag to gradually equate with the temperature of the pond or holding tank. After an hour, open the bag to let the fish swim free. Never drop a fish into the water. At first, a new fish will probably seek cover. Soon it will explore its new home and accept food.

FISH FOOD

A wide variety of fish food is available from your local pet shop. Feeding has never been easier or more convenient. Foods come in pellets, flakes, and tablets. Goldfish and koi prefer pellets and tablets that float or sink slowly to the bottom. Never feed flake foods to any pond fish since they pollute the water with their uneaten flake dust.

Foods may be dehydrated, frozen or livefoods. Different sizes are suitable for different sizes of fish. You can also prepare your own livefood cultures, as well as offer vegetable matter, table scraps, bread and dog chow to your fish, but it is wisest to stick to floating pool pellets.

Some foods are rich in carbohydrates. These compounds provide muscular energy. Other foods contain high concentrations of proteins. These produce vigorous growth and replace worn out muscle. Fats store energy, protect internal organs and act as insulation. Vitamins and minerals—vital aids in many bodily functions—are found in vegetables. These are found in different ratios in all foods, which is why a varied diet is crucial in maintaining good health.

TAMING

The pondfish can become quite tame if you feed them from a regular spot the same time each day. At your approach, the fish will become active as they anticipate a meal. Eventually, the fish will accept food from your hands. Some may even let you stroke them. Just be patient. Move slowly so as never to startle the fish.

Pond fish eagerly awaiting a meal. Feeding the pond inhabitants is an activity that can be enjoyed by all members of your family.

57

BREEDING

Although your fish may breed in the pond, the likelihood of any fry surviving is small. The youngsters are killed by disease, predators, and other fish in the pond.

Breeding in a pond is a hit-or-miss affair. You have no control over the male and female pairings. If you want to utilize selective breeding techniques, the chosen fish must be removed from the pond to a special tank or small pool. Here you are in control of the breeding and can ensure the survival of the young.

Select only those fish in the best health. Unfit adults will have less-than-vigorous young. Choose pairs that have good features that can be passed on to the offspring. Once you have made your selection, feed pairs extra amounts of protein and livefood.

It is difficult to distinguish between the sexes of goldfish. Generally, though, males are slimmer and more brightly colored. Male goldfish and koi in breeding condition display white spots, known as tubercles, on their gills and sometimes on the pectoral fins. Female fish appear swollen when viewed from above. This is due to the presence of the eggs within them.

Many fish breeders keep the sexes separated, but in sight of one another, for a few days before breeding. The pair is put in a tank with a glass divider. This situation increases their desire to breed. Also, some owners run two or three females with one male.

Both goldfish and koi are egglayers; fertilization takes place outside of the body. Furthermore, they are egg scatterers. As the eggs are spawned, they sink to the bottom of the pond. Some eggs may stick to plants or rocks. These fish have no parental interest in their young. Once the male has fertilized the eggs with his milt, the parents can be removed.

The temperature of the breeding tank should be about 2°C higher than the pond. The eggs will hatch in about four days. For two days the fry do not need food; they derive nourishment from their egg sac. Their first food will be brine shrimp, *Artemia salina*, or a similar fry-rearing food purchased from your pet shop. As the fry grow, offer them

Daphnia and other larger livefood.

It is important to cull poor specimens. Rearing a few, good quality fish is less expensive and results in better breeding than raising a lot of poor specimens.

Maintain accurate records of all the breeding activity. Include all information that will aid in a sound breeding policy, such as water temperature, feeding methods, quality of fry, parentage, etc.

HEALTH

Fishes, like all other forms of life, are susceptible to injury and disease. The severity and frequency of such ailments is dependent upon a number of factors, most of which can be influenced by the pond owner. The pond environment, the quality of food, the breeding program and the time of delay in taking remedial action are all significant factors in the health of your fish. You may not prevent your fish from ever becoming ill, but good husbandry keeps outbreaks to a minimum.

Spend as much time as possible with your fish. Monitor their appearance and activity on a daily basis. This way you can spot abnormal conditions in their early stages and take immediate action.

Some problems can be treated in the pond. However, it is best to treat fish on an

individual basis. Therefore, an isolation tank should be available for this purpose.

Internal problems do not always manifest themselves externally. If there are a number of unaccountable deaths of seemingly healthy fish, consult a vet for a post-mortem. Often only microscopy will reveal the problem.

As far as the well-being of your fish is concerned, preventive health maintenance is often far easier to achieve than a cure.

Seasonal Pond Management

Since a garden pond is an artificial creation, it requires special attention throughout the year. Careful monitoring helps to maintain a stable balance between the plants, fish, and water.

AUTUMN

As the leaves of deciduous trees begin to fall, cover your pond with a plastic mesh. This way the leaves are easily gathered and cannot sink to the bottom of the pond.

Remove dead leaves and old blooms from the aquatic plants. Trim back any rampant growth. Move delicate plants indoors for their winter hibernation. If you have some of the fancy goldfish varieties, transfer them to indoor tanks filled with water from the pond.

Remove as much debris as you can from drains and from the bottom of the pond. Use a vacuum pump specifically for ponds. Clear away surface algae with a fine net. Clean the filters and

pumps. Be sure they are greased and in good condition for future use.

As the temperature drops, reduce the amount of food given to the fish. Fish fed properly during the summer will have ample fat reserves for their winter rest.

WINTER

Reduce the output of the pumps, or turn them off altogether. It may be wise to relocate the pumps so that they are as close as possible to the filter outlet point. This will reduce the currents in the pond and help retain heat.

Another heat saver is to stretch clear polyethylene sheeting over more of the pond, much like a tent. Secure the edges well so it cannot be blown off by the wind. Sweep off any snow from the pond and the cover so that needed sunlight is not blocked.

Your fish will seek deeper and warmer water at the bottom of the pond. If your pond is less than 61cm (24 in) deep, bring the fish indoors. A pond of substantial depth should not freeze to the bottom, even though a layer of ice may cover the top. This ice covering retains heat in the lower layers. However, a solid ice cap inhibits the exchange of oxygen, so a hole should be provided. Never break the ice

Throughout the winter months your pond fish will undergo a period of dormancy. The food that they consumed during the summer will provide the necessary nutrients that their bodies need during this rest period.

At temperatures below 7°C (45°F), the fish will be just about stationary. They will not require any food. Very small fish, or those that do not look fit, should be brought indoors for the winter.

Life begins to stir in the pond as the temperature rises. The fish will start to feed, but slowly build up their meals to full rations. The increased warmth encourages the growth of algae, so the pond may look a bit cloudy. As the plants grow, the amount of algae should be reduced and the pond will clear. Increase the capacity of the pumps.

SUMMER

Activity is at its highest and the pond at its most beautiful during the hot days of summer. The pond should be deep enough that it cannot become too hot.

Also, there should be sufficient plants in the pond to provide shade. Predators like stagnant water with muddy bottoms. Therefore, keep the pond clean and the water circulating.

The more delicate species of aquatic plants should be removed from the pond and overwintered in a more suitable environment.

with a hammer or the fish may be stressed. Simply place a hot kettle on the ice until a hole is created. Or, you can buy a pond heater. These use up very little power. They keep just a small area of pond (around the heater) clear.

Large or small, fancy or informal, your garden pond can provide you with years of pleasure and satisfaction.

INDEX

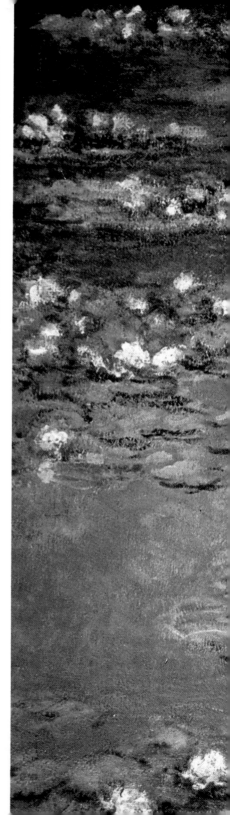